The Healing Power of Forgiveness

The Powerful Christian Series Book IV

THE HEALING POWER OF FORGIVENESS

By S. Richard Nelson

Other Books by S. Richard Nelson

Turning Faith into Power

Gaining Power through Prayer

The Added Power of Obedience

The Mighty Power of the Word

The Gift and Power of the Holy Spirit

Love: The Only True Power

Sustainable Spirituality:
Maintaining Faith in the Face of Adversity

The Faith Factor

5-star reviews are a blessing to Christian authors. If
you find this book inspirational, educational or simply
enjoyable, please post an honest review.

The Healing Power of Forgiveness

ISBN-13: 978-0-9904973-5-6
ISBN-10: 0990497356
BISAC: Religion / Christian Life / Spiritual Growth

Broken Hill Publications
Glenwood Springs, CO 81601

Edited by Stephen R. Gorton
Cover Design by Stephen R. Gorton and Connie Gorton

"From this broken hill,
All your praises they shall ring."
Leonard Cohen – *If It Be Your Will*

www.srnelson.com

"For God did not give us a Spirit of fear but of power and love and self-control."

2 Timothy 1:7

The Healing Power of Forgiveness

Table of Contents

The Healing Power of Forgiveness

*"Forgiveness is the fragrance
the violet sheds
on the heal that crushed it."*

The Healing Power of Forgiveness

Chapter 1

The Profound Power in Forgiveness

As one Roman soldier held Jesus' arm against the wooden cross, another soldier placed the point of a metal spike against the palm of Christ's hand, raised a wooden mallet and hammered the spike through the quivering flesh and into the cross. Had you, instead of Jesus, been the innocent victim, wrongly accused, unspeakably tortured and ridiculed, illegally tried and convicted and nailed to a cross to die, what would your mindset and attitude be as the nails tore through the flesh of your hands and

13

feet? The least likely human reaction is the very response that Jesus offered His crucifiers; the expression of His thought and heart was to petition forgiveness for those who had wronged Him. That is the power of Christ in the profoundest sense!

Repentance and forgiveness are the essence of the gospel of Jesus Christ. They are principles that offer hope, expectation and encouragement to every believer. As mortal humans living in a world of endless temptations and enticements, we can very easily make mistakes and commit sins. The atonement effected by Jesus Christ assures us that our slip-ups and missteps may be resolved through godly sorrow and by turning from our unrighteous ways.

The great blessing and miracle is that you and I, human and flawed as we are, have the very same power given to us. It is this inner power of forgiveness that changes lives. We are most like Jesus Christ when we forgive another person.

The healing power of forgiveness brings great joy and peace to us. This infinite miracle is a direct result of the great mediation and atonement of Jesus Christ. This reconciliation, where Jesus through His own choice paid the price of our sins and mistakes, sanctifies and purifies us. It is indeed the greatest miracle of all miracles.

Faith in Jesus Christ teaches us that it is worth everything to continually cleanse and purify our lives through repentance. It is because of our faith in Him that we have the power to receive His forgiveness.

Forgiving sin is a greater miracle and a more powerful act than healing the sick. Physical illnesses are a disease of the human body—visible, tangible, and apparent. Sin, on the other hand, is a disease of the soul and is invisible, intangible and not easily apparent. Jesus demonstrated His power not only to heal the sick, the lesser miracle, but to perform the greater act of forgiving sin. When a paralytic was brought to Him, Jesus saw his faith and said to him:

"'Have courage, son! Your sins are forgiven.'

"Then some of the experts in the law said to themselves, 'This man is blaspheming!'

15

"When Jesus saw their reaction he said, 'Why do you respond with evil in your hearts?

"'Which is easier, to say, 'Your sins are forgiven' or to say, 'Stand up and walk'?

"'But so that you may know that the Son of Man has authority on earth to forgive sins'— then he said to the paralytic— 'Stand up, take your stretcher, and go home.'

"And he stood up and went home." (Matthew 9:2-7)

Because of their weak faith, Jesus used the lesser power as evidence of the greater power He possesses. Why would He do this? Because the physical manifestation of healing an obvious illness offers proof in a more evident fashion. Forgiveness of sin is the greater miracle but because of their little faith, Jesus added the lesser miracle as proof of His power to also forgive sins.

We are all anxious to be forgiven of the mistakes we have made in life. Our mistakes may be matters of poor judgment, unintentional offenses, or any violation of God's law, but we can give our hearts over to the gentle impulses of the Holy Spirit and experience the refreshing renewal provided by God's forgiveness. Balance will then be returned to our lives.

Satan is determined to hinder every attempt we make to step off a wrong path and return to the narrow way that leads to eternal peace and happiness. But because we are ransomed through Christ, it doesn't matter how far we have gone down a wrong road, we can turn back.

Living in harmony with God is an important factor in a Christian's life. The Holy Spirit cannot dwell with us unless we are free of sin. Harmony with God is achieved when we conform to God's will, remembering that salvation comes through His grace. We experience this harmony only through the gift of Christ's suffering.

There was a time when I thought the Atonement was a done deal, that it took place as recorded in the New Testament and then it was over, accomplished, finished, and in one sense, at least, it is. The event took place. The ransom for our sins was paid. Jesus' own words spoken from the cross were "It is finished." But did His suffering forever end with His death on the cross?

After presenting Himself as the ransom payment for our depravity and failing, in pain and sorrow that is beyond our human perception, Jesus must still face the extreme sadness of observing God's children living out their lives being cruel, uncaring and conniving toward each other. Jesus regards us with compassion, aware of how desperately we need His grace and mercy, yet He suffers under the burden of recognizing that mercy and grace are unobtainable to those who lock Him out of their hearts and their lives. In this respect His suffering has continued beyond the garden, beyond the cross and even beyond the grave. Even now Jesus suffers.

And yet, He extends His love and mercy to all who reach out to Him. He isn't giving up on any of us. He does not refuse us forgiveness because our sins have become too great, too extreme or too numerous. On the contrary, He promises us that forgiveness is always there. This is the joyous news of the Gospel of Jesus Christ that He has the power to forgive.

The forgiveness offered to us through Jesus Christ is the essential element for achieving reconciliation with God and it contains three critical elements.

(1) We ask for forgiveness.

(2) We willingly forgive others.

(3) We receive forgiveness.

The ideal supplication for forgiveness is embodied in the Lord's Prayer. Jesus teaches us through His example to ask God to "forgive us our debts, as we also forgive our debtors." (Matthew 6:12) We cannot simply ask for forgiveness. We must first forgive those who have hurt or offended us.

If we separate the prefix from the root of the word "for-give," we discover that the precise connotation of the word is "to give in advance."

The Old English term *forgiefan,* a translation of the Medieval Latin word *perdonare*, means "to give wholeheartedly."

The Greek root means "to send forth."

The Hebrew root means "to carry away" or "to pardon or spare."

When we forgive someone, we carry away, send forth, or spare their burden of wrongdoing. We should do this totally, unequivocally and without resentment. Then, in like manner, we should accept the gift of forgiveness with genuine and honest appreciation. Real and sincere forgiveness restores harmony to the sinner as well as to the offended.

Jesus Christ, our Redeemer, loves us and has given us His gospel to protect us from taking the dark journeys in life. When we stray, repentance and the powerful gift of forgiveness have the potential to bring us back from those journeys, back from the depths of despair; and to bring us peace in this world and eternal life in the world to come. The purpose of this little book is to bring the strength and comfort of the Holy Spirit to all those who are reaching out for peace in a hurtful world.

Chapter 2

Sins as Scarlet

The fires of sin are tempting.

Have you ever sat around a campfire at night and watched as the moths and insects surround the flames in ever-enclosing concentric circles around the enticement of fiery light? Closer and closer they approach, orbiting and encircling the inferno until their perilous flight prompts a fatal mistake and they fall with scorched wings into the consuming flames of alluring enticement and temptation.

Humans are no different than those moths flirting with the tempting fires of sin. We want to experience the bright lights of sin and wantonness. We want to skirt the edges of depravity and debauchery. Oh, we may draw a line of distinction between sins like murdering, robbing or adultery, but we indulge in our favorite pleasant sins which we consider not so dangerous. We ignore the warning of the wise Alexander Pope who taught us that when abhorrent sin is "seen too oft" and we grow "familiar with her face, first we endure, then pity, then embrace." [1] We simply cannot encounter sin without polluting our minds.

Sin is any transgression of deific law. Sin is basically not conforming to a rule or law established by the Word of God.

Repentance means to turn away from sin. There are no successful sinners. We will all stand one day before God who will judge our obedience or disobedience and reward us accordingly. Ultimately there can be no success in sin.

---

[1] Oxford Dictionary of Quotations, p. 383.

True Christians and disciples of Jesus Christ must reconcile sinful behavior with their desire to become righteous followers, "for all have sinned and fall short of the glory of God." (Romans 3:23) John taught: "If we say that we have no sin, we deceive ourselves, and the truth is not in us. If we confess our sins, he is faithful and righteous to forgive us our sins, and to cleanse us from all unrighteousness." (1 John 1:8, 9)

All have sinned, but there is hope. When we feel disheartened and dispirited because of our failings, we have the great hope that the Lord is willing to forgive.

Most everyone has heard of Alcoholics Anonymous. If there were a "Sinners Anonymous" all of humanity would qualify for membership. We are all sinners. We are all in need of repentance. All of us have done something we shouldn't have done.

Sin is a heavy burden. In fact, it is the heaviest burden a human being can shoulder. Satan wants you to believe that once you have committed a sin there is no chance to come back into the Grace of God. But God tells us we can look to His son and live. We can repent and ask for forgiveness. When Satan wants to condemn us for our sins, Jesus tells us, "Neither do I condemn you. Go your way. From now on, sin no more." (John 8:11)

We are children of God and we are winged for heavenly flight. Very much like the dazzling light of a campfire, the hellholes of Satan can be very alluring. Just as a moth would be wise to avoid the bright flames, we must be careful not to make wrong choices in life. We should shirk the bright lights of sin.

The prevention of sin is always better than the cure and resisting evil requires applying gospel truth and knowledge. It is not enough to merely recognize and comprehend the ideologies that underlie God's great plan of salvation. We must utilize our learning to a stimulation of faith, so that when we are tempted, and trials come our way, we can draw from a reservoir of reserved spiritual power in times of stress and temptation.

Breaking God's law places us in Satan's grasp. The gospel of Jesus Christ is the perfect law of liberty and consists of commandments and edicts which free us from the ruler of the darkness of this world, (Ephesians 6:12) the enemy of all righteousness who, as the Master said, can "destroy both soul and body in hell." (Matthew 10:28)

When we are breaking or failing to keep one of God's commandments, we are in Satan's territory; and we become prey to impressions that spring from the lower region. By breaking the laws of the gospel, we are taking a sure step into the clutches of that cunning fiend, the devil, making it even easier for us to yield to additional temptations. One sin generally leads to another. The Apostle James asserted that: "whoever shall keep the whole law, and yet stumble in one point, he has become guilty of all." (James 2:10)

Paraphrasing what James said, if we offend in one point, and fail to correct it by getting ourselves back on track, it becomes easier for us to offend the next time temptation appears until finally we have offended in the whole law.

But if we repent we will be blessed because "blessed are those who mourn." (Matthew 5:4) The prophet Isaiah declared: "Though your sins be as scarlet, they shall be as white as snow; though they be red like crimson, they shall be as wool." (Isaiah 1:18)

We should repent daily. For the goodness of God to blossom in our lives, it must be nurtured and implemented through continual performance. If we want to be truly blameless, a daily pruning of our sinful nature through constant repentance is required. Scottish poet Robert Burns observed that "Saints are just sinners who keep on trying."

When we realize we have sinned we should recommit ourselves to living better. The depth of our remorse must be as deep as the sin we have committed. There is no easy way. It often hurts, but it always cleanses. Repentance will bring the greatest of all blessings; the forgiveness of God. We will no longer look back with depression and hurt but we will face forward into the future with faith, contentment and a love for God, for ourselves, and for all others.

Of course, once we have repented, Satan will want us to overemphasize, overstate and overstress our sinful pasts. This he will do to prevent us from focusing on future opportunities to grow and mature spiritually, and to love and serve others. We must remember that Satan is a miserable person and he wants to make us as miserable as he is.

Even though we are all imperfect human beings, we can learn to lift each other's sinful burdens and comfort others who need comforting. Our sinful natures and our weak characteristics can become our strengths if we humbly come to Christ in faith and receive his grace.

A beautiful story of forgiveness is recorded in Luke 7:36–50 involving a Pharisee named Simon, a woman identified as a "sinner," and Jesus. Simon had invited Jesus to come to his home and eat with him. After Jesus sat down, the woman, a sinner, began to anoint his feet with ointment. As she did so she wept, washing his feet with her tears, then wiping them with the hair of her head. Simon was offended when he saw the woman giving heartfelt attention to Jesus and said to himself that Jesus obviously wasn't really a prophet otherwise he would know what kind of sinful woman was touching him and would be embarrassed and repulsed and would not allow her to touch him.

Jesus perceived Simon's thoughts, and shared a parable with him.

"A certain lender had two debtors; The one owed him five hundred denarii, and the other fifty. When they couldn't pay, he forgave them both. Which of them therefore will love him the most?"

Simon thought it over and said: "He, I suppose, to whom he forgave most." Jesus answered: "You have judged correctly."

Then, while Simon seemed to want to dwell on the woman's sinful past, Jesus shifted focus, pointing out her present commendable acts. Extending certain courtesies to an honored guest, such as washing the feet, giving a kiss of greeting, and anointing the head with oil, was customary among the Jews in New Testament times. Jesus chastised Simon for his lack of common courtesies and noted for him that this sinful woman had washed his feet and kissed them and had anointed them with oil. Simon had failed to give Jesus water for his feet, had given him no kiss of greeting, and had not honored Jesus by anointing his head with oil.

Jesus then said: "Her sins, which are many, are forgiven, for she loved much. But to whom little is forgiven, the same loves little." Jesus then tells the woman: "Your sins are forgiven."

His final words to the woman were, "Your faith has saved you. Go in peace."

There is a magnificent lesson in this biblical episode. Since, as we noted in the beginning of this chapter, "all have sinned and fall short of the glory of God," all of us should put our sins behind us, like the woman at Simon's house, and then "go in peace" and not allow our sinful past to burden our souls.

Like Paul we can forget "those things which are behind." (Philippians 3:13) The Lord abhors sin, but he forgives the genuinely penitent. And then, even though our sins may be "as scarlet," we can still "go in peace," for the Lord, in his love, will make our sinful souls as "white as snow."

The Healing Power of Forgiveness

Chapter 3

The Healing Power of Forgiving Others

Forgiving others is often the hardest thing required of us by the gospel of Jesus Christ. Although it is sometimes difficult to implement, forgiveness is fundamental to peace in personal relationships.

As one unknown author explains: *"The first to apologize is the bravest; the first to forgive is the strongest; the first to forget is the happiest."*

We have a responsibility and obligation as followers of Jesus Christ to exercise the power of mercy and forgiveness toward others. Just as we receive forgiveness through faith on Jesus Christ, it is also through our faith that we can have the power to forgive others. All of which can be summed up in a single word—*grace*.

The elimination and expulsion of sin that emerge from repentance are only possible through the atonement of Jesus Christ. As we increasingly keep God's word we will receive "grace for grace" (John 1:16) In other words, we receive as much unearned, undeserved, unmerited grace from the Lord Jesus Christ as we are willing to give to others. The message of the Parable of the Unforgiving Servant as told in Matthew 18:23-35 teaches us that we receive grace from Christ in exchange for grace toward others.

The second great commandment tells us to love our neighbor, (Matthew 22:39) but love will not last without reciprocal forgiveness. Love simply cannot endure day-by-day without forgiveness.

The key element to spiritual health and well-being lies in learning to forgive and love others. Despite our own intense and earnest urge to be forgiven, the Savior ardently emphasizes the essential stipulation required to obtain forgiveness is to forgive others of their offenses toward us. Having a constant predisposition to forgive others is often an extremely difficult challenge, but to harbor the spirit of forgiveness in your heart and eliminate the spirit of hatred and bitterness brings peace and joy.

It is sublimely gratifying, when a sin has been committed by one person against another, to forgive that sin; and then, in accordance with the exalted and perfect pattern of Christ, to pray to our Father in heaven to also forgive the person who has offended us. As we attempt to forgive what others have done to us, we begin to let go of the sinful nature that has been difficult and challenging for us to forgive in ourselves.

Christ came to call sinners to repentance, to save them. Faithful Christians should be armed with mercy, despite the iniquities we endure. If one of us suffers, we should all feel it. Nothing will lead people to forsake sin as much as taking them by the hand and treating them with kindness. Jesus himself was condemned by the self-righteous Jews because He took sinners into His society.

The stipulation of forgiving others to be forgiven ourselves is a recurrent subject of holy scripture. Jesus directs us to pray, "forgive us our debts, as we also forgive our debtors" and emphasized the point by adding, "If you forgive men their trespasses, your heavenly Father will also forgive you. But if you don't forgive men their trespasses, neither will your Father forgive your trespasses."

Have you ever wondered about that connection? Why didn't Jesus simply tell us to ask to have our *own* debts forgiven? In one sense we are asking God to forgive us to the extent and only to the extent that we forgive others. Another way to look at it suggests that we are essentially saying: "Father, because I have reached that point in my life where I recognize that I am broken, because I have seen my weaknesses and my need for Your forgiveness, I want to forgive all others and that includes my enemies." (And here, perhaps, 'includes my enemies' might better be stated as '*especially* my enemies' because they are the ones that are bearing the heaviest burdens of unforgiveness). Jesus established that pattern of forgiveness and He is our perfect paradigm.

In the Gospel of John, scribes and Pharisees confronted Jesus with the woman "caught in the very act of adultery." Their impure and unrighteous intentions were to condemn the woman *and* to catch Jesus violating the law of Moses, but the Master defeated their duel objective without, at first, saying a word. Jesus "stooped down, and wrote on the ground with his finger, as if he didn't hear." (John 8:6) The Savior simply disregarded their insolent and offensive actions and accusations. Curtailing the shameful public 'hearing,' Jesus openly confirmed that the woman's sin would not prevent Him from loving the sinner.

The woman taken in adultery wasn't stoned to death for her sin because Jesus appealed to the conscience of those around Him. It is as though He were asking: "Who among all of you is truly justified?" Perhaps hoping to uphold what was left of the woman's dignity, Jesus stood and invited her accusers: "He who is without sin among you, let him throw the first stone at her."

Christ did not concede to the Pharisees' harsh and cruel demands but gave us instead an example of compassion, sensitivity and kindness when "again he stooped down, and wrote on the ground." The Savior's significant silence not only resolved the issue but also taught us a timeless lesson in human relations.

Jesus established both the sinner's infinite worth as well as her accusers' eternal value. He placed the woman's personal and private offense in its appropriate purview and He established that only "he who is without sin among you" can incriminate a sinner or refuse forgiveness to a wrongdoer.

Do you ever think of yourself as being without sin? After all, sin is such a serious word. It seems, at times, to be beyond the insignificant and mundane everyday wrongdoings of good-hearted Christians. We pride ourselves perhaps in having never done anything drastically wrong. But Jesus may just as well have said, "He who is without mistakes, failures, blunders, oversights, slip-ups, mis-steps, mix-ups, frustrations, hindrances, disappointments, in short, anyone who does not himself (or herself) need to be forgiven, let him first cast a stone." We must remember: "all have sinned and fall short of the glory of God." (Romans 3:23) Only Jesus is truly without sin in all its subtle shapes and sizes. Only Jesus does not need to be forgiven. And only Jesus can exact judgment and justice.

The efficacy of Jesus' reasoning is revealed in the crowd's response: "They, when they heard it, *being convicted by their conscience,* went out one by one, beginning from the oldest, even to the last. Jesus was left alone with the woman where she was, in the midst."

Jesus didn't point the finger. He didn't ask for evidence of the accusers' claim to reproach. In a candid act of genuine compassion toward both the accusers and the victim, Jesus simply places the problem back into the hands of those who created it.

When we stop throwing stones of sanctimonious self-righteousness, when we stop accusing, gossiping and classifying others as beneath us, when we love the sinner without loving the sin, our lives will flow with the serenity the Savior showed when He quietly "stooped down, and wrote on the ground."

Jesus' response to sin is a model for us all. His words to the woman, after her accusers had all left, are an indication of the woman's (and of all humankind's) worth: "Woman, where are they? Did no one condemn you? …. Neither do I condemn you. Go your way. From now on, sin no more."

A sinless Jesus suffered the sins of all to secure the privilege and power to forgive. To earn His forgiveness for ourselves, He requires that we also forgive others.

Whom exactly does He ask us to forgive?

Everyone.

How much does He require us to forgive?

Everything.

And for how long does he expect us to forgive?

All the time.

Once you have forgiven someone and that person deliberately and maliciously continues to transgress and offend against you, your response should and must be to continue to forgive. If you close the channel of forgiveness on another, you close the channel of love, compassion and forgiveness for yourself as well. When you have felt a measure of Christ's forgiveness in your life, but then turn and deny forgiveness to another, you alone become responsible for shutting off Christ's forgiveness toward you. Your unforgiveness has become worse than the other person's sin.

Christ did not deserve the suffering He endured. In many instances we do not deserve the misfortune and misery we suffer at the hands of others. Nonetheless, whatever has happened to us, we must forgive.

Admittedly, there are tragically grim offenses and sins committed against so many these days. Physical, emotional, and spiritual abuse is painfully and profusely perpetrated among family and fellow Christians. How do we pardon someone who has performed unspeakable harm and inflicted permanent damage to us?

We may, perhaps, understand the principle of forgiveness and even desire to fully practice it, but what we have gone through is far too painful. We are overcome by so much hurt. "I know I need to forgive," we may say, "and I really want to, but I just can't do it. I cannot forgive." Jesus' warning is sobering. If we don't forgive, neither will our Father forgive us. We may object thinking it's the other person who sinned. After all, we are the innocent victim!

Jesus was also the innocent victim. We aspire to be like Jesus. His forgiveness is divine. By forgiving others we are learning divine love. That is what we want on the great Day of Judgment: mercy, kindness, love, and forgiveness.

Do unto others as you would have Christ do unto you.

On our own, such Christ-like forgiveness would be nearly impossible against some of the sin we have faced at the hands of others. Only by calling on the power of heaven and drawing strength from the incomparable gift of the Holy Ghost can we do as Jesus did. With Christ's help we can rise above the sin of the sinner, withhold judgment, and demonstrate Christ-like love, kindness, mercy, and forgiveness.

The everlasting gospel teaches that to be forgiven, we must forgive. We cannot expect Heavenly Father to forgive us of all our sins if we withhold and refuse forgiveness to others.

Forgiveness is the most divine of all human attributes. Asking for forgiveness is the first step, but granting forgiveness is the most important. These actions wipe the slate clean, for both the perpetrator and the victim.

Sin is forgiven through faith in Christ. Anyone who, like the woman from Luke 7, has had the soil and suffering of sin washed away in the blood of the Lamb is going to love that kind and merciful God. Faith in the Lord Jesus Christ saves us, makes us whole, and brings us peace. We then belong to the family of Christ.

Our hope is for complete forgiveness of all our minor mistakes and errors as well as for all our deliberate sins and slip-ups. Life will present us with endless opportunities to learn to be like Jesus, and one of the most important godly qualities we can ever learn in life is to forgive— as Jesus does.

The Healing Power of Forgiveness

Chapter 4

The Healing Power of Forgiving Ourselves

The Christian life should be an adventure in forgiveness. Forgiveness is a wonderful healing gift which we need to give not only to others but to ourselves as well. Self-forgiveness frees us from self-punishment and empowers us to perceive the broader, more extensive possibilities of life beyond the confining gates of guilt or grudge.

The gospel of Jesus Christ can be summed up in two words: *repent* and *forgive*. Those two plain and simple procedures are the incomparable concern of any real Christian and they are a process of Christ's gospel that we can commence to live immediately.

To become all that God intended us to become, we must eliminate from our lives those things that are not God-like in nature. This can best be achieved through the gospel of repentance and forgiveness. The better we accept the gospel of Christ and recognize our own self-worth as children of God, the more we can forgive ourselves for our personal failings and shortcomings. Holding on to our past mistakes and failures can be detrimental to achieving our fullest potential as faithful Christians.

Paul attested to the Philippians that putting the past behind us and moving forward with faith is a principal step in our personal progress. He professed: "I do not consider myself to have attained this. Instead I am single-minded: *forgetting the things that are behind and reaching out for the things that are ahead.*" (Philippians 3:13) Paul acknowledges that he does not know all things, but he does understand the need to forget "those things which are behind," and to forgive ourselves for the things of which Christ has already forgiven

44

us. He evinces a compelling declaration that before we can reach "out for the things that are ahead," we must put our mistake-filled past behind us.

Nothing clutters the soul more than remorse, resentment and recrimination.

The benefits and blessings of self-forgiveness are numerous:

When we forgive ourselves for our own faults, failings and inadequacies, we begin the process toward conquering and defeating them. Instead of becoming paralyzed by a sense of our insufficiency, we acknowledge our faults and resolve them.

When we forgive ourselves for our own weaknesses, we respond toward others with more tolerant and accepting hearts. We adopt an attitude of acceptance, rather than accusation. In turn, we create a climate of trust and warmth in which relationships can flourish.

When we forgive ourselves for our own sins and shortcomings, we attract a spirit of peace within our hearts and our lives. It is the kind of divine peace celebrated in song: *"There'll be love and forgiveness, there'll be peace and contentment, there'll be joy, joy, joy."* [2]

Self-forgiveness is a wonderful practice! It is the psychological equivalent of a second chance. Self-forgiveness is permission to get up, dust ourselves off, and try again. It is the assurance that we are valuable and valued despite our errors.

We do not need to be sinless and perfect to be worthwhile and valued. The Greek dramatist Euripides noted: "Men are men, they needs must err." [3] Being human, we will stumble. Being forgiving of self and others, we will be forgiven.

The life of Bob McFarlane, a promising neurosurgeon, illustrates the power of self-forgiveness. During his residency, this devoted doctor began utilizing injected opiates to relax his overworked nerves. Before long, he became addicted and was debilitated by his dependency. He was expelled from his residency. For over a decade, he struggled to put his life back

---

[2] Natalie Sleeth, "Joy in the Morning," Hope Publishing Co.
[3] In Robert I. Fitzhenry, ed., *The Harper Book of Quotations,* 3rd ed. (New York: HarperCollins, 1993), p. 301.

together: sometimes trying to cure his addiction by himself and sometimes going in for professional treatment. After entering a long-term chemical dependency program, he finally started to make some real progress.

He credited his success to the power of self-forgiveness. He reflects: "My first hurdle was the overwhelming sense of shame and guilt at what I had done and the depths to which I had sunk. Two little phrases that I learned there aided in my deliverance from the bondage of guilt: 'He retaineth not His anger for ever, because he delighteth in mercy.' (Micah 7:18) and 'God has absolutely no attitude of condemnation toward man.' Armed with these I could now set about learning to forgive myself." [4]

Belief in God eventually translates into belief in oneself and McFarlane was finally able to find the power to beat his dependence. Faith in God was crucial to McFarlane's forgiving himself—and to his recovery. And now he helps many others do the same. After traveling the

[4] Lindsey Hall and Leigh Cohn, eds., Recoveries: True Stories by People Who Conquered Addiction and Compulsion (Carlsbad, CA.: Gurze Book Co., 1987), p.141.

long road to recovery, Bob McFarlane returned to the medical profession as a specialist in chemical dependency and a committed consultant to the Drug Enforcement Administration.

Bob McFarlane conquered his dependency and put his failures behind him, moving forward with faith. All of us can likewise achieve our greatest potential by believing in our strengths and by not being discouraged or consumed by our failures. It is said that Edison conducted more than 10,000 experiments before inventing the incandescent light bulb. He learned from failure, describing the events prior to his breakthrough as "10,000 discoveries of how electricity did *not* work." Edison turned his disappointments into discoveries and his failures into findings because he learned from his mistakes. He did not waste his life in self-condemnation for not getting things right the first time.

God has given each of us specific and uniquely defined strengths to aid in our personal development. Some may seem to have more skill and ability than others. Some may be farther along in developing their capacities and competence while others are at different stages of development, but one thing remains certain; we all have equal and unchanging worth in the eyes of a forgiving God. When we forgive, we have the glorious promise of being forgiven.

The Healing Power of Forgiveness

The Healing Power of Forgiveness

Chapter 5

Forgive to Be Forgiven

The process of forgiving another person often may require a seemingly unsurmountable effort but forgiveness is always the sure and reliable path to peace and healing. If you feel that you have been seriously wronged, if you are an innocent victim, don't harbor feelings of anger or hatred at the injustice. Honestly and sincerely forgive. (Mark 11:25)

If your offender requires discipline for a serious transgression against you, let the proper civil authorities handle the punishment and correction. Don't burden your own life with thoughts of retribution. God's mill of justice may grind slowly, but it grinds exceedingly well. No one will escape the consequences of the violation of God's laws. In His own time and in His own way, a full payment will be exacted for every unrepented evil act others commit against you.

Jesus' plea for us to stop hanging on to the sins of others in no way lessens the gravity of what the initial sinner did. And yet, He expects us to forgive so that when we need it, His forgiveness will also be available for us.

Forgiveness of that type is never easy or immediate. Depending on the gravity of the injustice, it might initially seem unattainable. But it isn't unattainable, or the Lord wouldn't have asked us to do it. I believe Christ is serious when He tells us to forgive others. He gave us His words because He means them. He is the ultimate example of saying what He means and meaning what He says. He has commanded us to forgive everyone! We need to find a way, and, if we ask, He will help us find that way.

Some offense is often merely a result of perception, which may or may not accurately reflect another's intentions. When we are accused of offending another, even if we are certain that we have not done so, we should simply ask for forgiveness. Asking for forgiveness demonstrates a genuine expression of trust in the healing power of forgiveness. It will begin a process through which the Holy Spirit can soften hearts and resolve issues before they become seemingly unsurmountable. Humility and a willingness to learn from our mistakes will bring tremendous benefits and blessings and can help us avoid serious misunderstandings.

Much of what we take as offense is merely miscommunication. Communication between humans can be extremely complex. A word's usual implication can be changed through inflection, tone, and body language. Past experiences can modify the meaning, connotation, and implied intent of phrases used in ordinary, day-to-day conversation.

An example will clarify what is meant. Shortly after we were married my wife said something to me. To this day I don't know if she misspoke or if I misunderstood, but my answer was not the appropriate one. No matter what my intent had been, she was convinced that I meant to be offensive in my response. It became reality for her.

We must be aware that what is innocently said can, under the influence of Satan, become raw material for a quarrel, an acrimonious exchange, a destroyed friendship, or a ruined relationship. No wonder the Prince of Peace admonishes every soul to show forbearance and quickly and candidly forgive.

We should continually practice the principles of kindness and mercy and be ready to forgive each other at the first sign of repentance and whenever forgiveness is sought from us. If we were to forgive each other, and even our enemies, before they repent or ask for our forgiveness, our heavenly Father will be equally as forgiving and merciful toward us.

We can pray for our enemies, both Christian and non-Christian, and not look for retaliation against those who oppose or offend us because "Vengeance is mine, I will repay, says the Lord." (Romans 12:19)

A simple apology to a spouse, a parent, a co-worker, or a friend who has wronged us could be the key to free us both. Apologies are invaluable in helping us lay down our burdens and move ahead with life and with living. An apology can heal another and mend a relationship in ways nothing else can and, in the process, we can arise a bit more as children of God.

Children caught in altercations with one another often defend themselves by exclaiming, "He started it!" (I often used that technique myself). But God doesn't care who started it. He is, however, very concerned about eliminating conflict between people. He clearly tells us to be reconciled with others *before* coming to Him. If you hope to come to Christ or if you wish to present yourself at His altar, and you "remember that your brother has anything against you," you are told to "leave your gift there before the altar, and go your way. First be reconciled to your brother, and then come and offer your gift." (Matthew 5:23, 24) We can then present ourselves before Christ with full purpose of heart, and He will receive us.

Is it true that we really can't see Him until we are reconciled with others? If you thought that a lack of forgiveness or apologies was keeping you from coming closer to Christ, wouldn't you want to resolve that issue immediately?

Jesus charged us to unreservedly forgive. Peter posed the question that most of us have probably asked at some time or another: "Lord how often will my brother sin against me, and I forgive him? Until seven times?" (Matthew 18:21) We have all probably wondered when we can stop forgiving someone for a repeated offense. At certain moments, we would like to write our own formula for justice. There have been moments when each of us has probably wanted to stop forgiving, to stop turning the other cheek and instead go for the jugular.

But the Lord makes clear to Peter, and to all of us, that our responsibility is to be forgiving, and that justice and mercy are His responsibility. He responded to Peter's query, "I don't tell you until seven times, but, until seventy times seven." (Matthew 18:22) As a child, I used to impishly multiply seventy by seven to justify that I only had to forgive someone 490 times! I now have a better understanding of the saving implication of Jesus' counsel: We are to forgive without limit and without price. He paid the ransom for our sins and paid the cost of our penance. Only He can determine when we have forgiven too much, too mercifully or too many times.

It has been suggested that perhaps Jesus wasn't giving us a specific number that we should adhere to but rather was suggesting that if we have not yet forgiven our offenders seventy times seven, then it may very well be that we have not forgiven them once.

Empathy is an important attribute to help us avoid misunderstandings and offenses, as well as to facilitate forgiveness. (Ephesians 4:32; Colossians 3:13) Empathy helps compensate for our lack of full understanding of what others are going through in their personal lives, in suffering, in anxiety, in wrestling with problems that they may feel helpless to resolve.

Often all a person needs is a listening ear; someone who is willing to take the time to be attentive. We sometimes feel we may not be able to help others and don't know how to resolve the challenges they face, yet our kindness may give them courage to continue. In so doing we can help them increase their faith in the healing power of the Savior, just because we were willing to listen attentively.

Jesus promised that the merciful shall find mercy. We should seek to help save souls, not to destroy them: "I tell you that there will be more joy in heaven over one sinner who repents, than over ninety-nine righteous people who need no repentance." (Luke 15:7)

Many of us act as if forgiveness and repentance were only for good Christian people like ourselves. It's almost as though we say, "Oh, she's basically a good person, so I guess I'll forgive her." But what about those who have caused us physical, emotional, mental, or spiritual suffering? What about those who have broken almost every gospel law and commandment, bringing pain and conflict into our lives through their sinful choices? Do we have to forgive them?

We do.

We cannot pick and choose whom we will forgive, based on our own standard of forgive-ability. The Lord will judge us with the same measurements meted out by us. If we are harsh toward others, we can expect harshness from Him. If we are merciful with those who injure us, He will be merciful with us in our errors. If we are unforgiving, He will leave us weltering in our own sins.

So be forgiving.

Chapter 6

Forgive and Forget

After a workplace altercation, an offended woman, offering the physical motions and mouthy words of reconciliation and forgiveness toward a co-worker, turned to her employer with anger-filled eyes and remarked, "I'll forgive her, but I have a memory like an elephant. I will never forget what she did."

A feigned forgiveness is valueless and void. Henry Ward Beecher expressed the thought: "I can forgive but I cannot forget is another way of saying I cannot forgive." When we continue to embrace bitterness or attempt to rebuild our relationship bridges with a pretended pardon, we continue to live without the peace of mind forgiveness affords. True forgiveness must be an unreserved purging of all bitter feelings and thoughts. Mere words avail us nothing.

"But if you don't forgive men their trespasses, neither will your Father forgive your trespasses." (Matthew 6:15)

One of the greatest qualities of any Christian is forgiveness. When we can forgive others for real or imagined trespasses against us, then we, too, can be forgiven for our trespasses. Someone has said: "Humanity is never so beautiful as when praying for forgiveness, or else forgiving another."

It is always easier to talk about forgiveness than to practice it, especially when we are victimized by another's mistake. Forgiving and forgetting is the hinge around which all interpersonal progress revolves. Many people, when attempting a reconciliation with others, say that they forgive, and yet they hold on to malice, mistrust and skepticism.

Reconciliation and repentance should bring about forgiveness as well as forgetfulness. It is important that we forgive others their offenses, but it is essential that we release any ill feelings and not allow the matter to smolder or fester. To be acceptable to the Lord, true forgiveness entails forgetting. As implied in Christ's model prayer, "forgive us our debts, as we forgive our debtors," it must be a heart action (forgive) and a purging of the mind (forget).

At times it can be extremely difficult to forgive those who have injured us. We tend to dwell on the evil others do to us. That constant agonizing soon becomes a distressing and destructive canker. Like a life-threatening cancer, an unforgiving attitude eats away at our soul and disturbs our energy and existence.

The wrongs inflicted on us can be petty or extremely painful, simple or sensational, but when we refuse to follow Jesus' counsel to forgive (whether forgiveness is asked for or not) we invoke greater pain and sorrow for ourselves and eventually become emotionally debilitated. Only Jesus' redemptive surgery is strong enough to prevent or treat such a disease.

Often the ones who wronged us do not even suffer. They may be entirely unaware of the hurt they have caused. Even when they are aware of an offence and their consciences are piqued, their pain is seldom as damaging as the self-inflicted sores produced by an attitude of unforgiveness.

Forgiveness means forgetting. What if Jesus rejected us on the frivolous and petty things we do to others? What if Jesus held a grudge for every hurt we ever caused Him? How much mercy and grace could we expect from Him? We certainly should be merciful toward each other and overlook simple and small offences. If we are hanging onto a grudge, some bitterness, disappointment, or jealousy, we should let it go. We cannot control what others do, but we can control our own hearts and minds.

When feelings get hurt, when mistakes have been made, and when wrongs have been committed, we can forgive. Forgiveness can be very difficult. We hurt over the wrongs instigated against us. But the hurt can be healed. Regardless of how deep the cut or sensitive the sore, we can find the strength to forgive in the healing power of Jesus Christ.

Forgiving and forgetting requires extreme inner strength and Christ-like love. Our ability to forgive and forget is a measure of our spiritual maturity. We are all God's children and we all need the benefit of repentance and forgiveness that comes through Christ. We have the undeniable responsibility to repent and the unequivocal obligation to forgive; and to forget. Forgiving and forgetting are such essential components of the gospel of Jesus Christ that we cannot walk the difficult road of life without these redeeming doctrines.

In *The Scarlet Letter*, Nathaniel Hawthorne reveals how the Puritan community prevents Hester Prynn from putting the sin of adultery behind her by causing her to wear a scarlet A on her chest. (Imagine if you had to wear a symbol of all your sins for everyone to see and condemn for the rest of your life!) In time, Hester becomes a great asset to the community, a noble nurse and a benevolent doer of good deeds, but the Puritanical culture still insists she wear the scarlet letter.

Eventually, some of these Puritans become so appreciative of Hester's services that the letter A she wears ceases to be a symbol of adultery to them. Instead, for the forgiving few, it symbolizes everything from "able" to "angel." Hawthorne writes: "The letter was the symbol of her calling. Such helpfulness was found in her, so much power to do, and power to sympathize, that many people refused to interpret the scarlet A by its original signification. They said that it meant Able; so strong was Hester Prynn, with a woman's strength." [5]

For the forgiving and forgetful few who saw Hester's A as an emblem of all her virtuous behaviors, they found a true and compassionate friend and took comfort in the scarlet letter's promise of forgiveness. For those few, "The scarlet letter had the effect of the cross on a nun's bosom."

Thankfully, we no longer label sinners with scarlet letters, but all of us engage in a subtler sort of condemnation when we refuse to forgive by not forgetting others' offences. Our human natures tend to want us to label everyone by the wrong they have done or the hurt they have caused. But no matter how much

---

[5] Hawthorne, Nathanial, *The Scarlet Letter*, in Norton Anthology of American Literature, 2nd ed. (New York: W.W. Norton & Co., 1985), pp. 1193-94.

we have been hurt, nothing good comes from unforgivingly labeling another's sins.

If we slapped a letter on our parents' forehead for every mistake they made, or a letter for every time our brother or sister hurt us, or a letter for every unkindness from a co-worker, or a letter for every injury from a friend, or a letter for every unfeeling act of a spouse, all our foreheads would become so cluttered and encumbered, loaded and laden with resentment, anger and hurt. The labels of our mistakes would prevent us from recognizing the value and worth of the person behind those mistakes.

We can't control what others say or do. We can't reverse another person's wrongdoing. But we can regulate how we respond to their mistakes and misconduct. We can refuse to equate the error with the individual by remembering that what someone does is separate from who that person is. We may not like their performance, but we can still like the performer. It's been said that "the human soul seldom rises to such heights of strength and nobility as when it removes all resentments and forgives errors and malice."

When we refuse to forgive another, we are tearing down the very bridge that we must also cross. Jesus taught this truth in the parable of the unmerciful servant who demanded forgiveness but was merciless in forgiving another. (Matthew 18:23-35). We cannot hold grudges and unkind feelings without harming ourselves. Holding on to grudges we hurt ourselves more than we hurt our offenders. The Apostle Paul wisely counseled, "Don't let the sun go down on your wrath." (Ephesians 4:26)

Bitterness poisons the one who holds it in his heart. It generates hatred, and "everyone who hates his fellow Christian is a murderer, and you know that no murderer has eternal life residing in him." (1 John 3:15)

In Victor Hugo's, *Les Misérables*, the main character, Jean Valjean, steals some food for his hungry family in a moment of desperation. He is caught, imprisoned and forced into almost twenty years of hard labor. This experience makes him hardened and bitter. After his release a bishop treats Jean kindly, but Jean repays this kindness by stealing the bishop's silver. Police soon catch Jean in possession of the bishop's silver and haul him back to the bishop's home to confess his thievery. Jean fully expects to be severely punished and subjected to another even longer prison term, but the bishop looks at the silver, smiles, and treats his traitor like a friend. He explains to the police that he gave the silver to Jean Valjean, and then he baffles Jean, pointing out that he forgot to take the silver candlesticks that were also intended for him. This act of forgiveness and charity deeply moves Jean Valjean, melting away his bitterness and causing him to literally transform his life.

For Jean and for us, the healing power of forgiveness can create a powerful transformation in the life of the forgiven as well as of the forgiver. An attitude of forgiveness will radically alter the way we perceive others. A forgiving approach to life accepts that people can change. It helps us see the good around and within us. It can motivate others to become more Christ-like and forgiving.

The effect is cyclical: the more we forgive in others, the more others will forgive in us, and the more eagerly God forgives us, and the more we can then forgive ourselves. As the Lord says: "If you forgive men their trespasses, your heavenly Father will also forgive you." (Matthew 6:14)

Our forgiveness should be weighted on the side of mercy. Jesus implored, "Therefore be merciful, even as your Father is also merciful" and "Blessed are the merciful, for they shall obtain mercy." (Luke 6:36, Matthew 5:7) Nowhere in Jesus' teachings are we advised to take the law into our own hands, to right the wrongs committed against us or to have all our injustices and injuries resolved. Jesus fulfilled the law of Moses which admonished an "eye for an eye, and a tooth for a tooth." Christ's counsel is to turn the other cheek. (Matthew 5:38)

One of the heaviest loads we can carry is a grudge. James warns us against holding grudges toward others: "Do not grumble against one another, brothers and sisters, so that you may not be judged. See, the judge stands at the gates!" (James 5:9) Amid the discordant sounds of hatred, resentment and revenge conveyed so deafeningly these days, the soft and subtle song of forgiveness can be a healing balm for the forgiver as well as for the forgiven.

Revenge and retaliation are entirely foreign to the gospel of the gentle, forgiving Jesus Christ. Through the healing power of forgiveness, we put our human failings aside and demonstrate a more divine identity. We create heavenly connections in our human relationships when we practice the principle of forgiveness. When we rely on the redeeming power of the atonement, we recognize the universal worth of God's children.

Retaliation is not repentance. Paul told the Romans: "Do not repay anyone evil for evil; … Do not avenge yourselves, dear friends, but give place to God's wrath, for it is written, 'Vengeance is mine; I will repay,' says the Lord." (Romans 12:17, 19)

God judges our thoughts as well as what we say and do. He knows the intent of our hearts. We do not possess this ability. We hear what people say, we see what they do, but cannot discern what they think or intend. Consequently, when we attempt to fathom the meaning and motives behind the actions of others and interpret their intentions, we can often judge wrongfully.

Jesus clearly and emphatically declared:

"Do not judge so that you will not be judged.

"For by the standard you judge you will be judged, and the measure you use will be the measure you receive." (Matthew 7:1, 2)

The principle of not judging others is not a once-and-it's-done deal. It is a day-by-day requirement of the Christian life. Jesus tells us to clean up our own lives first—to remove our beam-size faults, before we turn our attention to the shortcomings of another.

"Why do you see the speck in your brother's eye, but fail to see the beam of wood in your own?

"Or how can you say to your brother, 'Let me remove the speck from your eye,' while there is a beam in your own?" (Matthew 7:3, 4)

A speck is a tiny sliver, but a beam is usually a great, strong timber used to support the heavy roof of a building. If we are weighed down with beam-size sins, it would certainly be wrong to point out the sliver of sin in someone else. Our vision becomes completely obscured when we ignore our own faults and look only for the foibles of others. If we worked harder on correcting our own weaknesses, we would realize that the sins of others may be so much smaller in comparison.

We should not harbor hatred against anyone, Christian or non-Christian. God is love. Jesus illustrated the necessity and the importance of forgiving others if we also want to be forgiven. When he was crucified at Golgotha—the cruelest kind of torture—suffering intensely though innocent, he did not ask God to take revenge on the perpetrators, but asked his Father in heaven, "Forgive them, for they know not what they do." Imagine Him pleading for their forgiveness while He was under such intense suffering on the cross! That is the true Christian example for us. We should avoid allowing ill-feelings to fester in our hearts and extend the same forgiveness to each other.

As we begin to overlook what offenses others have committed against us, we can begin to release all that has been difficult to forgive about ourselves. Forgiveness can become the key to peace in our personal relationships. If we can somehow wipe the slate clean and see everyone as blameless, we can also begin to see ourselves as blameless. We will feel peace.

The greatest virtue that we can employ in our lives is the virtue of forgiving and forgetting.

Chapter 7

Return Good for Evil

It only seems logical that the greatest sermon that was ever preached, by the greatest man who ever lived, would give us the greatest counsel that we could ever live by. In that important sermon known as the Sermon on the Mount, Jesus advises us that, instead of engaging in our usual conflicts and retaliations, we should return good for evil. To most of us that recommendation might sound a little strange. It is the opposite of the prevalent procedures of hate, argument, and retaliation most of us live by.

Among other things taught that day, Jesus told His followers:

"You have heard that it was said, 'Love your neighbor' and 'hate your enemy.'

"But I say to you, love your enemy and pray for those who persecute you,

"so that you may be like your Father in heaven." (Matthew. 5:43-47)

This idea of returning good for evil is a part of that great philosophy of the Golden Rule which says: "In everything, treat others as you would want them to treat you." (Matthew 7:12)

Suppose we were to take this doctrine of the Master teacher seriously about returning good for evil and consequently see if we can't make our own lives more meaningful. Treating other people kindly makes sense for several reasons. The good that we do to someone else is like bread cast upon the water; it always comes back to us greatly increased. Even so, we don't always follow this advice very well.

The lowest and most unprofitable form of human response to any situation is that of returning evil for evil, or even evil for good. Even though we know that no one ever wins in a war, people continue these less profitable methods of responding to others. Individually, we continue to get angry, to argue, to dislike people, while being completely aware that no one ever gets ahead that way. If we were to follow Christ's directions and develop the attitudes that allow us to return good for evil, then we could take credit for being true Christians, and we would discover how to handle every situation so that it becomes pleasant and profitable for both sides.

Not all of us have the provision to forgive another by replacing bad with good. We are often hurt by people in whom we see little good at all. We may see the offender as being only bad and committing nothing but harmful, hurtful acts. In such instances, it may be necessary to search faithfully for the good qualities deep within those unpleasant people. Good qualities and values can eventually be found in most everyone.

Spinoza expressed that: "He who wishes to revenge injuries by reciprocal hatred will live in misery. But, he who endeavors to drive away hatred by means of love, fights with pleasure and confidence; he resists equally one or many men, and scarcely needs at all the help of fortune. Those whom he conquers yield joyfully, not from want of force, but increase thereof."

Andrew Carnegie tells us that we may have to "mine for the gold" in some people. "You must literally move tons of dirt to find a single ounce of gold…. You do not look for the dirt, you look for the gold." Sometimes we must remove a ton of sin to find the gold within certain people. Sometimes we must extract a lot of protective covering. Sometimes we may even need to explore our own inner caverns of misconduct. In any case, we will be able to replace bad with good when we dig deep enough to discover the wealth of human potential, the reservoir of worth, to which all of God's children have claim.

Since the beginning of time, humans seem to have a greater affinity for the opposite philosophy in which we pay off our enemies with a greater dose of evil. Husbands attack their wives and wives retaliate against their husbands. Democrats downgrade Republicans and Republicans do the same to Democrats. Even religion strikes out at other religions. The world has violent battles on several fronts almost continually.

When we return evil for evil, we end up with broken homes and bankrupt lives, we suffer from all the hate and anxiety that our actions incur. And yet we continue to cling fiercely to the disappointing practice where we persist in paying everyone off in his own coin.

Jesus said: "You have heard that it was said, 'An eye for an eye and a tooth for a tooth.'

"But I say to you, do not resist the evildoer. But whoever strikes you on the right cheek, turn the other to him as well.

"And if someone wants to sue you and take your tunic, give him your coat also.

"And if anyone forces you to go one mile, go with him two." (Matthew 5:38-41)

The more we resist and do battle with our enemies, the harder they fight against us and the more hate-filled we become. When we attack them, they hit back at us. When we demean them, they debase us. Remember that before we can hate someone else, our own heart must also be filled with hate. The failing philosophy of an eye for an eye carried to its conclusion would eventually end up making all of us blind.

An opposite example of this philosophy is illustrated by a story from the golden age of ancient Greece. A mugger once attacked the great statesman Pericles and subsequently, put out one of his eyes. The young man was arrested and, according to the ancient Grecian law, turned over for punishment to the one he had harmed.

Consequently, Pericles was given full authority over the violent young man. He could have had him immediately slain or he could have made him his slave for life. He could have taught him a lesson, making him a public example by giving him some of his own medicine; he could put out one of the young criminal's eyes. But the great Pericles did none of these things.

Instead, he took the young man into his home and taught him kindness, patience, love, respect for law and order, and a love of truth and right. He taught him that kindness is better than violence, that love is better than hate, and that reason is better than arguments. Many years later, when the young man was completely reformed and had developed a passion in his soul to be like his benefactor and help people instead of hurting them, Pericles gave him back to society as an honorable, worthwhile citizen.

Even before Jesus put this idea into words, Pericles was aware of the divine law of returning good for evil, and he returned kindness, love, and generosity for the violence, hatred, and rebellion he had received from the young hoodlum. He also gave him a good example of how someone formed in the image of God should live.

We might sometimes think that Jesus' counsel of loving our enemies, blessing those that curse us, doing good to those that hate us, and praying for those that despitefully use and persecute us as being merely something to discuss in Sunday School but with little value for life's actual situations. But this is not so. In these few sentences Jesus has outlined a philosophy of human relations that provides us with one of the finest codes of conduct ever put into words. When we accept this philosophy, we are given a substantial advantage in life. On the other hand, if we reject Jesus' counsel and fail to make this beneficial philosophy a part of us, we suffer a serious loss in life.

Once we have accepted Christ into our hearts and had our sins forgiven, we retain that forgiveness by forgiving others and by a lifetime commitment of charitable conduct. Returning to our sinful selves after our initial remission of sins is comparable to the return of leukemic blood cells after the initial remission of the disease. Leukemia is a malignant disease caused by the uncontrolled growth of leukocyte precursors in blood, bone marrow and certain body tissues.[6] Proper treatment will often bring this life-threatening disease into remission, eliminating the cancerous, malignant blood cells.

Much of the world today suffers from a spiritual leukemia. The diffusion of sin destroys

---

[6] The Nelson Textbook of Pediatrics (1143).

the soul just like the dissemination of leukemic blood cells destroys the body. The spread of sinful conduct in our lives can be brought into remission when we accept Christ. Our new state of spiritual well-being requires that we forsake sin and embrace righteousness.

Spiritual leukemia is a form of pride. The insightful Christian writer, C. S. Lewis, has commented: "For pride is spiritual cancer: It eats up every possibility of love, or contentment or even common sense." [7] Meekness is an aspect of all our virtues. Pride is an aspect of all our sins.

The insidious encroachment of pride into our lives impairs our desire to forgive and to return good for evil, inhibiting us from removing sin from our lives. This spiritual cancer can only be brought into remission and be effectively eliminated from our souls through faith in Jesus Christ. In experiencing our spiritual rebirth and the accompanying change in our hearts, we retain in remission the cancerous pride and sin that could otherwise infect our souls.

---

[7] Lewis, C. S., *Mere Christianity*. New York: Macmillan, 1960.

We retain a remission of our sins by remembering the greatness of our God, praying daily, and standing steadfast in the faith of Jesus Christ. Retaining a remission of sins is as vital to spiritual life as retaining a remission of cancerous leukemic blood cells is to physical life.

Although the counsel to return good for evil may seem simple and straightforward, its eternal consequences are of paramount importance. When we accept Christ, we enter in at the gate of the path that leads back to God. But it was never intended that we stand around lingering at the gate. Jesus expects us to move forward along this path. He marked the path and led the way He intended us to follow. Jesus descended below all things so that He could ascend above all things and declare: "I am the way." (John 14:6) His declaration assures us that we won't need to walk the path alone, but we will need to walk.

When we return good for evil, we facilitate our progression along the path that leads back to God. The word most commonly used to describe the actions of people pursuing this path is love. It is the pure love that never fails. (1 Corinthians 13:8)

In one of his books, Robert Fulghum describes the following event which took place in Oslo, Norway, on the tenth of December 1980:

"A small, stooped woman in a faded blue sari and worn sandals received an award from the hand of a king…. In a great glittering hall of velvet and gold and crystal. Surrounded by the noble and famous in formal black and in elegant gowns. The rich, the powerful, the brilliant, the talented of the world in attendance. And there at the center of it all—a little old lady in sari and sandals. Mother Teresa, of India. Servant of the poor and sick and dying. To her, the Nobel Peace Prize.

"No shah or president or king or general or scientist or pope; no banker or merchant or cartel or oil company or ayatollah holds the key to as much power as she has. None is as rich. For hers is the invincible weapon against the evils of this earth: the caring heart. And hers are the everlasting riches of this life: the wealth of the compassionate spirit." [8]

---

[8] Fulghum, Robert. *All I Really Need to Know I Learned in Kindergarten*. New York: Villard, 1989.

Is there any doubt that retaining a remission of sins depends on caring for one another, loving our enemies, blessing those that curse us, doing good to those that hate us, and praying for those that despitefully use and persecute us? If we believe these teachings, if we profess to follow Jesus, if we are true Christian disciples, then we must do the things that the Savior said and did. He said: "Most assuredly I tell you, he who believes in me, the works that I do, he will do also." (John 14:12)

Grecian mythology tells us about Midas, the king of the little Greek state of Phrygia, who was granted an unusual gift in which everything that he touched turned into gold. It must have pleased Midas to go around touching worthless objects and to see them transformed into beautiful, valuable, shining gold under his touch. Jesus has given us a greater and even more important gift. By following his instructions to return good for evil, we will also acquire a golden touch that can change ugliness into beauty, worthless people into valuable children of God, and all the miseries and failures of life into the pure gold of joy, success, and righteousness.

The Healing Power of Forgiveness

5-star reviews are a blessing to Christian authors. If you found this book inspirational, educational or simply enjoyable, please post an honest review.

About the Author

Rich Nelson is the author of over 45 published works on topics such as religious education, family values, health, and politics. His writing has appeared in *Christian Education Today, Church Teacher, Parish Teacher, Living with Teenagers, Liberty Magazine,* and many others.

Contact Information:

Broken Hill Publications
Glenwood Springs, CO 91601

Email Rich at: rich@srnelson.com

Visit Rich at: www.srnelson.com

The Healing Power of Forgiveness

Other *Powerful Christian* Books by S. Richard Nelson

Turning Faith into Power
Book 1 of The Powerful Christian Series.

Turning Faith into Power is the first in a series of instructive and inspirational books from The Powerful Christian Series by S. Richard Nelson. The Savior says in Matthew 17:19-20, "For most assuredly I tell you, If you have faith as a grain of mustard seed, you will tell this mountain, move from here to there, and it will move; and nothing will be impossible to you."

What mountains would you remove from your life if you had the faith of a mustard seed? What's stopping you from removing the obstacles in your life? Do you utilize your faith as a principle of action and power? Is your faith centered where it will be most effective? Do you have adequate faith in yourself?

As believing Christians there is substantial power available to us. It is the power of faith. Through the bounteous mercy and love of Jesus Christ we receive his grace - a divine means of strength. The power available to us through Jesus Christ is very real.

Gaining Power through Prayer
Book 2 in The Powerful Christian Series

Sincere prayer is a fountain of divine power flowing into our lives. Through prayer we gain clear and precise direction. Through prayer we access the strength of character to perform God's will – to do what is right. Prayer is the process we use to place ourselves in contact with God.

The impressive power of prayer warrants the consideration not only of Christians, but of all societies. This little booklet highlights the principle applications and purposes of prayer. It confirms that God does answer our prayers and demonstrates how we can be more aware of those divine answers. It also examines the challenging question of why, at times, it appears that God does not answer us and what we can do about it.

The Added Power of Obedience
Book 3 in The Powerful Christian Series

Two opposing powers grapple in every human heart and our decisions are usually influenced by them, either to do good or to do evil. The spirit of truth will always persuade us to obey God. We all want happiness. We hope for it, live for it, and make it our primary goal in life. But do we live in a way that allows us to enjoy the happiness we desire so deeply?

The way to be happy is simply to believe in Jesus Christ and obey the gospel. When we obey God's law, then we can expect to find the happiness we desire. Obedience to God is not an inconvenience, it is our ultimate aspiration; it is not a stumbling block, it is a powerful and profitable building block.

The Healing Power of Forgiveness

www.ingramcontent.com/pod-product-compliance
Lightning Source LLC
Chambersburg PA
CBHW070544030426
42337CB00016B/2336